Apostle Melvin E. Moore

There Is

A

CALL

In The Land

To

FOCUS

BECAUSE

Society is Caught in a Web of Distraction

This book or parts thereof may not be reproduced in any form or by any means without written permission from the publisher, except brief passages for purpose of reviews.

Scriptures quotations are taken from The Holy Bible New King James Translation (NKJV), copyright @ 1982, The Life Application Bible New International Version (NIV), The Living Bible copyright@ 1971, The Holy Bible King James Version copyright @2005

Interior Illustrations by Ms. Gabriel Crumpler

Published by: Grace Us Living Publishing

Copyright © 2016 by Melvin E. Moore

Library of Congress Control Number: 2016952961

ISBN: 978 0 9832187-3-9

All rights reserved.

Printed in the United States of America

CONTENTS

DEDICATION

ACKNOWLEDGEMENT

FOREWORD

A PASTOR'S REFLECTION

INTRODUCTION...11

CHAPTER ONE...15
The Call to FOCUS

CHAPTER TWO...22
FOCUS Movement

CHAPTER THREE...27
FOCUS Is the Key

CHAPTER FOUR...37
Social Media
Helped Develop Distractions

CHAPTER FIVE...42
When Distracted Blink and FOCUS

CHAPTER SIX...50
Pitfalls of Wandering

CHAPTER SEVEN...54
The Caterpillar Understands FOCUS

CHAPTER EIGHT...58
FOCUS on the Body

CHAPTER NINE...74
Tough Vs TOFF

CHAPTER TEN...92
It Is Time to Shift Our FOCUS

CONCLUSION...103

ABOUT THE AUTHOR

LET'S KEEP IN TOUCH

REFERENCES

DEDICATION

This book is dedicated to The New Generational Church that is on the Rise.
They will run with a new mindset and carry the FOCUS Movement Torch, now and in future generations.

ACKNOWLEDGEMENTS

To God, for trusting me as His mouthpiece and instrument to declare "There Is a Call in the Land to FOCUS, Because Society is Caught in a Web of Distractions."

To my loving wife, Dr. Margaret H. Moore; for your prayers, patience and partnership through the many years. You have been my spiritual warrior, encourager; given me inspiration and strength, through good and bad times.

To my children, grandchildren and great-grandchildren and all that you add to my life.

To every person who have prayed, encouraged and contributed in the writing, research, illustrations and every added component to this project.

To my Kingdom Connection Christian Center Family, local and worldwide: Thank you for allowing me to serve.

FOREWORD

As apostles and pastors, we have come to realize that there are many in the church today who have been distracted by the many ills in our society and in life. Melvin Moore's new book, "There is a Call in the Land to Focus, Because Society is Caught in a Web of Distractions", will bring about a new awareness of the need for us to focus and refocus. He said it best, "the world is in a web of distraction."

Focus will allow you to get rid of those distractions, and live the life that God intended for you to live. What you focus on will manifest in your life. *"Set your affection on things above, not on things on the earth."* (Colossians 3:2)

Our focus on the Word of God will cause heaven to manifest here on earth. Focus allows us to 'on purpose' make our way prosperous and have good success. *"This book of the law shall not depart out of thy mouth; but thou shalt meditate therein day and night, that thou mayest observe to do according to all that is written therein: for then thou shalt make thy way prosperous, and then thou shalt have good success."* (Joshua 1:8)

Focus is meditating on what God has said and not what we see naturally. We are supernatural beings. We can see beyond what we see naturally. "There is a Call in the Land to Focus Because Society is Caught in a Web of Distractions" will help you discover your supernatural ability to refocus to focus.

Focusing on the Word will change the way you think. Your thinking will change your actions, and your actions will change your life. If you do not change the way you are thinking, your thinking will change you.

"Above all, be careful what you think because your thoughts control your life." (Proverbs 4:23)

When we focus on God's Word consistently, we will no longer be controlled by the ills of society or life; but will begin to manifest God's plans and purposes for our lives.

Apostle Tony and Cynthia Brazelton,
Victory Christian Ministries International VCMI, Suitland Maryland,

A PASTOR'S REFLECTION

Dear Reader,

Surely, Apostle Melvin Moore has tapped a master key in the Kingdom of God with this revelation concerning the importance of focus.

From the very beginning of time, it becomes clear from the narrative of the scriptural account of the history of God's plan for man. Man's focus on God's Words and ways, were paramount to the life of blessing that He had in His design. In fact, the law of sin and death began to rule in the heart of man. God's alternative to keep man from building a tower to the sky, independent of Him, was to destroy their unified focus by confusing their language. The Tower of Babel is proof that the dominion of man is unlimited when he or she is unified in focus. He said concerning their endeavor, *"Look,"* he said. *"The people are united, and they all speak the same language. After this, nothing they set out to do will be impossible for them!"*
(Genesis 11:6)

Once distracted, their potential and plan was thwarted. Men were unlimited before the confusing of their language distracted their focus. This event in Genesis 11 took place after the law of sin and death entered the world. Imagine what a born again, spirit filled, kingdom man or woman can do, if they will bring their lives into focus by meditation in God's Word.

Apostle Melvin Moore has captured this kingdom law, and put it in focus for the reader. It is a must read for anyone who wishes to navigate the end-time demonic distractions of this age, and achieve their full potential in Christ. Read away and put this Kingdom revelation into practice. It has been a blessing to me and it surely will be a blessing to you.

"Now to Him Who, by (in consequence of) the [action of His] power that is at work within us, can [carry out His purpose and] do superabundantly, far over and above all that we [dare] ask or think [infinitely beyond our highest prayers, desires, thoughts, hopes, or dreams] (Ephesians 3:20)

In HIM,

Pastor William Tracy Harris,
Harvest International Ministries

INTRODUCTION

The Word of the LORD for this season: "There is a Call in the Land to FOCUS Because Society is Caught in a Web of Distraction." What is your distraction? In applying the Word of God, it is of the upmost importance that we understand this principle. Our life cannot be changed until we change what we know. Therefore, it is evident that it is not only what we know, but what we do with what we know.

The church is experiencing a great Apostasy, as well as, a great exodus of people from the Word of God. The body of Christ is getting away from sound doctrine. They are becoming a people with itching ears of man's wisdom, while denying the power of the Holy Spirit. It is time to FOCUS on the Word of God.

Now the Spirit expressly says that in latter times some will depart from the faith, giving heed to deceiving spirits and doctrines of demons.

(1 Timothy 4:1)

However, our FOCUS is going to revolutionize society again by captivating the more abundant life. FOCUS is a right now Word that will cause one to receive, and make the right decision the right time. It is not always necessary you will need a confirmation from somebody to confirm what GOD has already said to YOU. Selah! If a boomerang is thrown out, where is it destined to return? Therefore, FOCUS becomes personal and it starts with you first. Yes, it is time to FOCUS!

Entering the world of FOCUS through this book, we will explore and identify one of many distractions in the world today. Each chapter is filled with empowering FOCUS Keys needed to help answer the call. FOCUS is all that we see in the Word.

For by faith we understand that the worlds were framed by the word of God, so that the things which are seen were not made of things which are visible.

Hebrews 11:3

FOCUS will give society and the body of Christ, the ammunition needed to answer the call to FOCUS and finish His work.

Now finish the work, so that your eager willingness to do it may be matched by your completion of it, according to your means.

2 Corinthians 8:11

Stay focused and locked-in as you continue to read this book.

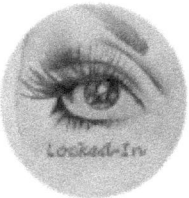

THE WEB OF DISTRACTION

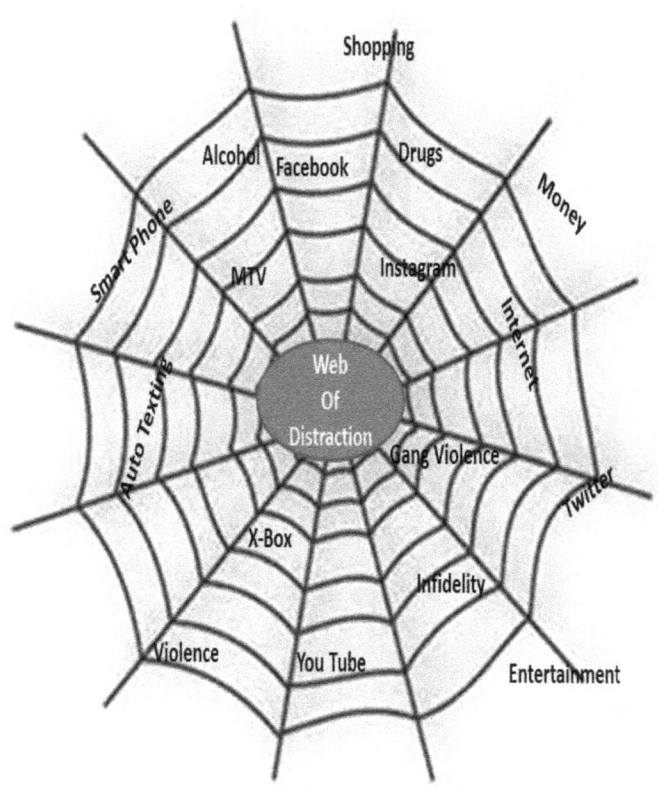

CHAPTER ONE

THE CALL TO FOCUS

In September of 2014, I was awakened from a normal and regular night's sleep. I continued to lay in the bed, as I often do, meditating on the Word of God. God began to minister to me. These are the words He spoke to me while staring at the ceiling. He said, "There is a Call in the Land to FOCUS Because Society is Ccaught in a Web of Distraction." In my mind, I wondered, "God what are you saying." He continued, "Society is caught in a web of distraction. Many people are turning their FOCUS on everything, other than My Word. The church too, have been caught in this web of distraction, mainly through the power of Social Media."

There are many Social Media platforms. There are ways it is very useful and helpful to society and the church. However, when these platforms take away the time of studying the Word of God, it becomes a distraction. It has disguised itself as quality time in our day to day fellowship with God. The answer lies in becoming focused!

Study to shew thyself approved unto God, a workman that needeth not to be ashamed, rightly dividing the Word of truth.

2 Timothy 2:15

FOCUS is the key in staying connected to our foundation and creator. It is through this connection; we may live a more abundant life. God called me to bring awareness to society and the body of Christ through this book about "FOCUS". It will guide the church back to sound doctrine and principles of the Word of God. There is a level of FOCUS we must tap into in this season. Doing so, will eliminate distractions that will keep the church from its destiny and purpose.

I was given two foundational scriptures for this season of FOCUS to apply to our life:

Trust in the Lord with all your heart, and lean not on your own understanding; In all your ways acknowledge Him, And He shall direct your paths.

Proverbs 3:5-6

Therefore, my beloved brethren, be steadfast (FOCUS), immovable, always abounding in the work of the Lord, knowing that your labor is not in vain in the LORD.

I Corinthians 15:58

God later gave me the acronym for the word "FOCUS". The meaning expresses who we are as sons of God, made in His very image. FOCUS is '**F**ull **O**f **C**onsistent and having **U**nlimited **S**ight' in the Word of God.

Jesus is our example. He was so **C**onsistent that He would only do what His Father would have Him to do. Jesus had **U**nlimited ability, **S**ight and access in what God wanted Him to accomplish. Every believer has inherited that same ability. As three part beings, we are a spirit, we have a soul, and we live in a body. The same spirit that raised Jesus Christ from the dead lives on the inside of you and I; when we accept Him as our Lord and Savior. Therefore, the Holy Spirit that lives in every believer gives us the ability to have, and be '**F**ull **O**f **C**onsistent and have **U**nlimited **S**ight' in the Word of God, FOCUS.

It is crucial that we understand the true power of FOCUS. It is having the supernatural ability to perceive, receive and live in God's blessings. We are required to develop a 'Lifestyle of FOCUS.' Think about this: Whenever there is success in our life, it is usually because we remained focused. When there is defeat in something that we can accomplish, it is because of distraction. FOCUS is the key. FOCUS is for me. It is all that we should see. We are '**F**ull **O**f **C**onsistent **U**nlimited **S**ight' in the Word of God, and not the world. We must remain FOCUS to receive the more abundant life.

I can recall days after receiving the Word from the LORD about bringing awareness to the body of Christ to FOCUS. He began to work with me daily to prepare messages through various conversations going forward. God gave me a series of messages on FOCUS from September 2014 through August 2015. The messages ministered to our congregation. As a result, our ministry is growing to become '**F**ull **O**f **C**onsistency and **U**nlimited **S**ight'. We are witnessing transformation in their family lives, on their jobs and in the market place.

I can remember one morning. I set out to organize the kitchen. I should have begun by taking the dishes out of the dishwasher. Instead, I sat at the table with my wife, and began working on an upcoming message for Bible Study. The original plan before entering the kitchen was organizing the kitchen. Immediately, the Holy Spirit spoke to me and said, "Do not be distracted, take the dishes out of the dishwasher, and finish cleaning the kitchen." I said to myself, "WOW, how quickly I allowed myself to be distracted, and recognized the importance of staying focused." From that encounter, I began to understand the level of FOCUS needed in our lives daily. How full and complete we would be if we followed through with what the Holy Spirit places in our spirit to do, and carried it out daily? We would experience the more abundant life.

God used another incident regarding my wife being **F**ull of **C**onsistency and obedience. There was a time when she was very sick, and scheduled to minister at Bible Study that night. I told her I could do it, but she said, "I will make it." Then I said to her, "What are you trying to prove?" She did not respond. We went to bible study. In her obedience to God, and her consistency in carrying out her assignment, the anointing of God moved mighty through her that night like never! Why? I believe because she was focused on her purpose in ministering the Word of God. She was not distracted by the pain and discomfort in her body.

Months later, God told me to write this book and a song on "FOCUS." The song is titled "CR (Call and Response to FOCUS)." The base scriptures are:

Trust (FOCUS) in the LORD with all your heart, and lean not on your own understanding but in all your ways acknowledge Him, and He shall direct your paths.

Proverbs 3:5-6

Therefore, my beloved brethren, be steadfast (FOCUS), immovable, always abounding in the
work of the LORD, knowing that your labor is not in vain in the LORD.

1 Corinthians 15:58

FOCUS is the key to understanding the signs of the times. The "sons of Issachar" understood the signs of the time, and what Gods' people should do to overcome distractions. Thus, we would have **C**onsistent **U**nlimited **S**ight in what God has called us to do. Therefore, God spoke to me to bring awareness to society and the church.

There is a call in the land to FOCUS because society is caught in this web of distraction. Therefore, FOCUS becomes the key to the abundant life.

FOCUS KEY

FOCUS is the key in staying connected to our foundation and creator, that we may live a more abundant life.

PAUSE

Write down what God just said or is saying right now in this chapter!

_____

_____

_____

_____

Stay focused and locked-in as you continue to read this book.

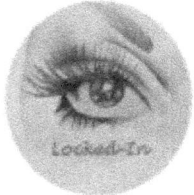

CHAPTER TWO

FOCUS MOVEMENT

I believe the church is entering another moment in this generation, and experiencing the power and manifestation of God like never. There have been many Christian movements in times past in the body of Christ.

First, there was the modern '24-7 Prayer Movement.' It is a movement spanning denominations and focusing on the pursuit of God as the FOCUS of one's life. The International House of Prayer in Kansas City, MO is a visible example of this concept called the 'Charismatic Movement.' This is a movement which Pentecostal beliefs and practices spread to churches outside of the Holiness tradition. The 'Charismatic Movement' is the international trend of historically mainstream congregations adopting beliefs and practices like Pentecostals. Fundamental to the movement is the use of spiritual gifts. Among Protestants, the movement began around 1960, and among Roman Catholics. It originated around 1967.

Now there are diversities of gifts, but the same Spirit. There are differences of ministries, but the same Lord. And there are diversities of activities, but it is the same God who works all in all. But the manifestation of the Spirit is given to each one for the profit of all: for to one is given the word of wisdom through the Spirit, to another the word of knowledge through the same Spirit, to another faith by the same Spirit, to another gift of healings by the same Spirit, to another the working of miracles, to another prophecy, to another discerning of spirits, to another different kind of tongues, to another the interpretation of tongues. But one and the same Spirit works all these things, distributing to each one individually as He wills.

1 Corinthians 12:4-11

That is the distribution process of spiritual gifts.

Next was the 'Confessing Movement.' It is a neo-Evangelical movement within several mainline Protestant churches. Its mission was to return those churches to what members see as greater theological orthodoxy.

If we confess with our mouth, and believe in our heart that Jesus died on the cross, and was raised from the dead, something happens. We are saved.

Romans 10:9

Third, there was the 'Grace Movement'. This movement began in the 1930s, and embraced the Mid-Acts Position Dispensational System of Bible interpretation. It properly applies a Protestant doctrine that basically views the teachings of the Apostle Paul. Both were as unique from earlier apostles. It also views as foundational for the church, and a perspective sometimes characterized by proponents as the 'Pauline Distinctive.'

In theology, a dispensation is the divine administration of a period of time, a divinely appointed age. Dispensationalist is a theological system that recognizes these ages ordained by God to order the affairs of the world.
Dispensationalists believe that God is in this age; and is focusing His attention on the church. He will again, in the future, FOCUS His attention on Israel.

Currently, there is another movement in the body of Christ. It is moving in our society, from city to city, state to state, and nation to nation. This movement focuses on the pursuit of God as the FOCUS of one's life. It is called the 'Movement to FOCUS'. This movement is what this book is about. The FOCUS Movement started, October 2014 in Fayetteville, North Carolina at Kingdom Connection Christian Center Church International. The year 2014 will be the next dispensation of time, a divinely appointed age. The FOCUS Movement goal is to identify the distractions that have trapped many in our society and the church.

Let us look at society through the Web of Distractions. In this Web, many react more heavily on their feelings, rather than the spirit man that lives on the inside. Many distractions are attached to Social Media. It seems, everyone want to expose their life before the world. Politics, gang and gun violence, gambling, money, shopping, drugs, and alcohol. You fill in the blanks!

The 'Movement to FOCUS' is the key to having the more abundant life. It enhances families, work relations, advancement and eliminates division in race relations. FOCUS establishes our morality that will bring this society back to a society of love and respect for one another.

FOCUS KEY

True FOCUS moves beyond the natural into the supernatural.

Set your mind and keep FOCUS, habitually on the things above (the heavenly things), not on things that are on the earth, which have only temporal value.

Colossians 3:2

PAUSE

Write down what God just said or is saying right now in this chapter!

_____

_____

_____

_____

Stay focused and locked-in as you continue to read this book.

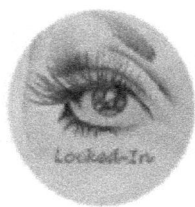

CHAPTER THREE

FOCUS IS THE KEY

We are in a season where we must begin to understand our situations. Solutions to problems are determined by the keys used to lock and unlock issues in life. Choosing and having access to the right keys will bring about the more abundant life. The right key is FOCUS. Keys only purpose in life is to gain access and close out penetration (lock and unlock).

Jesus answered and said to him, "Blessed are you, Simon Bar-Jonah, for flesh and blood has not revealed this to you, but My Father who is in heaven and I also say to you that you are Peter, and on this rock, I will build My church, and the gates of Hades shall not prevail against it. And I will give you the keys of the kingdom of heaven, and whatever you bind on earth will be bound in heaven, and whatever you loose on earth will be loosed in heaven."

Matthew 16:17-19

Keys are no more than pen and pencil. David reminds us,

My heart is overflowing with a good theme; I recite my composition concerning the King; my tongue is the Pen of a ready writer."

Psalms 45:1

    There is a safe place where we can address the issues we face. That safe place is called FOCUS. We must FOCUS on the spirit man on the inside of us. That Spirit is called the "Holy Spirit." FOCUS is the key that solidifies our relationship with God.

Therefore, my beloved brethren, be steadfast (FOCUS), immovable, always abounding in the work of the Lord, knowing that your labor is not in vain in the Lord.

1 Corinthians 15:58)

Blessed is the man who walks (FOCUS) not in the counsel of the wicked, nor stands (FOCUS) in the way of sinners, nor sits in the seat of scoffers; but his delight (FOCUS) is in the law of the LORD, and on his law, he meditates day and night.
He is like a tree planted by streams of water that yields its fruit in its season, and its leaf does not wither. In all that he does, he prospers.

Psalm 1:1-6

We must continue to FOCUS, and be not distracted.

For those who live according to the flesh set (FOCUS) their minds on the things of the flesh, but those who live according to the Spirit set (FOCUS) their minds on the things of the Spirit.

Romans 8:5

Finally, brothers, whatever is true, whatever is honorable, whatever is just, whatever is pure, whatever is lovely, whatever is commendable, if
there is any excellence, if there is anything worthy of praise, think (FOCUS) about these things.

Philippians 4:8

FOCUS is meditation.

This Book of the Law shall not depart from your mouth, but you shall meditate in it day and night, that you may observe to do according to all that is written in it. For then you will make your way prosperous, and then you will have good success.

Joshua 1:8

We have our eyes on everything. However, God desires to have our FOCUS on Him. FOCUS is the key in eliminating distractions. It is defined as a concentrated effort or attention on an aspect of a thing. By revelation from the Holy Spirit, FOCUS means that we are **'F**ull **O**f **C**onsistent and **U**nlimited **S**ight' in the Word of God. Jesus was so consistent that He said,

"I will only do what my Father would have me to do."
Then Jesus said to them, "When you lift the Son of Man, then you will know that I am He, and that I do nothing of Myself; but as My Father taught Me, I speak these things."

John 8:28

FOCUS moves us through a door. It is only revealed to those who hunger and thirst after His righteousness.

But seek ye first the kingdom of God, and his righteousness; and all these things shall be added unto you.
Matthew 6:33

Through our FOCUS, we will discover the mysteries of His will for our life. The word "discover" means to make known or visible, to expose, display (place before us), to obtain sight or knowledge of, for the first time.

But we speak the wisdom of God in a mystery, even the hidden wisdom, which God ordained before the world unto our glory.

1 Corinthians 2:7-8

The wisdom of God would be to understand that FOCUS is the key to eliminate the distractions and experience the more abundant life.

FOCUS IS A JOURNEY

The journey starts now! It is a journey from one vision to the next. The path leads us to our purpose. Undoubtedly, along the way, we will have challenges. Challenges will develop perfection, and perfection develops levels of success. Our FOCUS must become spiritual.

While we look (FOCUS) not at the things which are seen, but at the things which are not seen: for the things, which are seen are temporal; but the things which are not seen are eternal.

2 Corinthians 4:18

Where there is no vision (FOCUS) the people perish; but he who keeps the law blessed is he.

Proverbs 29:18

Focus is key when allowed or permitted to operate in the mind. Embrace your mind. The mind is incredible. It is our number one tool we have. God created us to use it in the world. Everything about setting goals, making plans, being productive and improving focus, starts in the mind. Having a sharp mind is extremely valuable. It helps you to function in this world, and do what you do. The mind helps us become successful.

Bishop TD Jakes asked a question at a seminar, "Are you really being effective, or is your life cluttered with all kinds of stuff that demand you, drain you, tax you and stop you, from being your highest and best self? Are you substituting busyness, and all the chaos that goes along with busyness from being effective?"

To be effective, we must become focused. That means to FOCUS or '**F**ull **O**f **C**onsistent having **U**nlimited **S**ight' in the Word of God. Jesus was so **C**onsistent, He only did what His Father told Him to do. God placed Adam and Eve in the garden to bring order. Instead, they
became distracted because they were not focused. This resulted in order not being carried out. Therefore, humanity suffered. When we are focused on the Word of God and carry it out, we have transitioned into God's Order.

ORDER

O= Obedience In
R= **R**ight **S**tanding
D= making a **D**ecision
E= that is **E**ffective
R=in its **R**elease in the earth

Let me remind society and the church, FOCUS was in the beginning! The world was created because the earth understood, it must FOCUS on the commands from God. The earth was so focused on every Word that came out of the mouth of God. They were so focused, that when He spoke, the earth "focused" on it and brought it to pass. For the next seven days, the earth worked hand and hand with God's commands. Through focusing on what God commanded, it brought forth manifestations that are the foundation of this world. The earth did not just hear, but it moved out on what it heard.

But be doers of the word, and not hearers only, deceiving yourselves, For if anyone is a hearer of the word and not a doer, he is like a man observing his natural face in a mirror; for he observes himself, goes away, and immediately forgets what kind of man he was. But he who looks into the perfect law of liberty and continues in it, and is not a forgetful hearer but a doer of the work, this one will be blessed in what he does.

James 1:22-25

In the beginning, God created the heavens and the earth. The earth was without form, and void; and darkness was on the face of the deep and the
Spirit of God was hovering over the face of the waters.

Genesis 1:1-2

When God began to speak, the earth was so focused on His commands that it focused on every word that came out of His mouth and carried it out.

Note: We must FOCUS on what God is saying to our spirit, and not allow our head to get in the way.

Then God said, "Let there be light"; and there was light, and God saw the light that it was good; and God divided the light from the darkness; "The Earth focused on the light and carried it out"

Then God said, "Let the waters under the heavens be

gathered together into one place, and let the dry land appear." "The earth focused on the water and carried it out." From this point until completion, the earth focused on what God said and carried it out.

Then God said, "Let Us make man in Our image, according to Our likeness; let them have dominion over the fish of the sea, over the birds of the air, and over the cattle, over all the earth and over every creeping thing that creeps on the earth." So God created man in His own image; in the image of God He created him; male and female He created them. Then God blessed them, and God said to them, "Be fruitful and multiply; fill the earth and subdue it; have dominion over the fish of the sea, over the birds of the air, and over every living thing that moves on the earth."

Genesis 1:26-28

Therefore, we must become focused on what God has entered our minds to do and carry it out. God carried out what He heard in His mind to do, and by the spirit of God we must carry out a spiritual command from God to do.

Therefore, I say then: "Walk in the Spirit, and you shall not fulfill the lust of the flesh."

Galatians 5:16

FOCUS KEY

FOCUS is being locked in, and God has the key. FOCUS is like a laser that locks in on the target, eliminating distractions.

PAUSE

Write down what God just said or is saying right now in this chapter!

_____

_____

_____

_____

Stay focused and locked-in as you continue to read this book.

CHAPTER FOUR
SOCIAL MEDIA HELPED DEVELOP DISTRACTION

Society and the church are caught in a Web of Distraction called Social Media. It is one of the leading causes of distraction in society today. Social Media is defined as forms of electronic communication. Users create online communities to share information, ideas, personal messages, and other content. The problem began when Social Media took our FOCUS from the Word of God.

Some Social Media platforms include:

- Social networking sites- Facebook and Google Plus. Many faces are on Facebook more than in the BOOK!
- Micro-blogging sites- Twitter causes one not to be quick to listen and slow to speak. (James 1:19)
- Publishing tools- Word Press, Blogger
- Collaboration tools- Wikipedia; "Study to show thyself approved rightly dividing the Word of truth." (2 Timothy 2:15)
- Photo sharing sites- Instagram falling in love with oneself, and not Christ Jesus.

- Video sharing sites- YouTube, Vimeo and Selfies- There was a song that said "You Don't Have to Be a Star to Be in My Show" by Marilyn McCoo & Billy Davis Jr..
- Personal broadcasting tools- Blog Talk Radio, U-Stream and Live-Stream. It seems Live Stream causes some to stay at home; being distracted from fellowship in corporate settings.
- Snap Chat

Instead of spending much of our time distracted by Social Media, our time should be focused on the Word of God. There is victory in God's System and His Word.

GOD'S WORD IS A SYSTEM

The acronym for a system is the result of God's process.

S-Standard
Y-You
S-Should
T-Take
E-Even
M- Mimic.

Therefore, become imitators of God. Copy Him and follow His example. as well-beloved children imitate their father and walk continually in love [that is, value one another—practice empathy and compassion, unselfishly seeking the best for others], just as Christ also loved you and gave Himself up for us, an offering and sacrifice to God [slain for you, so that it became] a sweet fragrance.

Ephesians 5:1-2

TWO TYPES OF SYSTEMS

Perfect and Established Systems

Perfect System: God System is a Perfect System and if focused, illuminate's distractions and divisions.

Established System: They continued steadfastly in the apostle's doctrine, and fellowship in the breaking of bread, and in prayer. Acts 2:42

GOD'S WORD IS A SEED THAT CAUSES:

S-Success
E-Established
E-Every
D- Day

A seed was planted at Pentecost called the Holy Spirit, and a seed continued as the Apostle doctrine. God's Word causes success to be established in our lives every day.

As long as the earth remains there will be seed time and harvest.

Genesis 8:22

FOCUS KEY

The problem began when Social Media took the place of FOCUS from the Word of God.

PAUSE

Write down what God just said or is saying right now in this chapter!

_____

_____

_____

_____

Stay focused and locked-in as you continue to read this book.

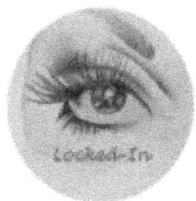

CHAPTER FIVE
WHEN DISTRACTED BLINK AND FOCUS

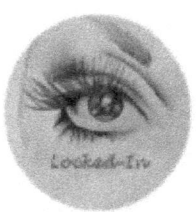

There are times when our visual FOCUS becomes distorted. The normal reaction would be to vigorously blink, wipe and refocus to gain clear FOCUS. The enemy is a master of disguise and deception. Therefore, to be effective in the Kingdom of God, we must see what He sees, and challenged to do like Jeremiah.

Moreover, the Word of the LORD came to me, saying, "Jeremiah, what do you see?" And I said, "I see a branch of an almond tree." Then the Lord said to me, "You have seen well, for I am ready to perform My Word."

Jeremiah 1:11-12

To BLINK: To close your eyes for a very short time, and quickly open them again. Society is called to "Refocus"

To FOCUS: To adjust your vision so that you see clearly and sharply, or become adjusted for clear vision. Our goal should be to always FOCUS on the Word of God.

Seek first the Kingdom of God and His righteousness, and all these things shall be added to you.

Matthew 6:33

FOCUS is being 'locked in' and having tunnel vision. Our eyes are the windows to the soul. When we…

'BLINK and FOCUS'

It will clear out the distractions. When we open our eyes and blink, it causes a tearing of the eyes that clears out the trash in our eyes. This causes clear sight to come forth.

Clear out self that feels I have failed; because it was not exactly the way I wanted it to be.

Clear out what I see happening now and FOCUS on what God said before.

Note: God created the retina of the eye to be stimulated by objects. Light helps to generate certain things so the brain can register the images.

It all started with God. He is our Creator. Next, we can see, when we open our eyes. What we see is based on how we receive, and what we do with what we see. The things we see could be positive or negative. Therefore, how we see should be based on the way God sees. We should be looking through the spiritual eyes of God. Our perception of things should line up with Gods' Word. When we view things negatively, and with the wrong perception, we are not seeing properly.

We do not look (FOCUS) at the things which are seen, but at the things which are not seen. For the things, which are seen are temporary, but the things which are not seen are eternal.

2 Corinthians 4:18

The human eyes are a gift from God. God is the creator of everything. He gave us eyes for **S**ight, and we need to FOCUS our eyes on Him. From time to time, our physical eyes need to adjust darkness, light, eyewear, binoculars, shapes, colors, 3D pictures, TV screens and much, much more. As a follower of

Christ, we need to make the necessary adjustment to our spiritual eyes. This adjustment helps us to refocus on God; who is the Light of the World. With His **S**ight, we are **F**ull **O**f **C**onsistent **U**nlimited **S**ight in His Word; seeing everything in perfect **S**ight. Instead of focusing our eyes on our problems, circumstances and cares of the world, we will cast our cares on the Lord.

Therefore, my beloved brethren, be steadfast (focus), immovable, always abounding in the work of the Lord, knowing that your labor is not in vain in the Lord.

1 Corinthians 15:58

What God has for the church is foundational, when we partake of it. The five virgins were focused and heard the call. The others became distracted and missed the call. It is paramount that we are ready to receive what God have for us always. God is saying to His people…

'BLINK and FOCUS'

It will clean out the trash that makes us feel that we have failed in life. You have not failed! Begin by cleaning out the past.

During one's journey, imperfections may interrupt your thoughts along the way. However, you can still enjoy what God is doing in your life. You may have made a few mistakes, but whatever happened or did not happened,

'BLINK and FOCUS'

God has built a safe and productive environment that is tailored for you and I to…

'BLINK and FOCUS'

Get back to doing the things of God. He is calling and waiting. He wants society and the church to rest in Him. God wants us to lean on Him for understanding. He wants us to realize that when we cast our cares on Him, all our anxieties, worries and concerns will be taken care of. We must give them to Him. Yes, He cares and have the deepest affection for you. He always watches over each of us very carefully. Yes, we can…

Cast our cares on Him, for He cares for us.

1 Peter 5:7

As a Pastor, I want to offer you hope, so that your life can change and get better. There is a safe place that you can address the issues you face.
That safe place: 'FOCUS' on the Word of God.

F= Full
O= Of
C= Consistent
U= Unlimited
S= Sight

FOCUS is a safe-haven. Being focused will place a shield around your thought process. It protects negativity from penetrating our mind. FOCUS causes one to filter out the very thing that causes distractions, and gives us the ability to meditate on what is important. There is a life that God desires for us, but we must use the spiritual tools to receive it.

Among whom also, we all once conducted ourselves in the lusts of our flesh, fulfilling the desires of the flesh and of the mind, and were by nature children of wrath, just as the others.

Ephesians 2:3

To implement this spiritual tool and achieve the life that God desires for us to live, we must FOCUS on our spirit.

FOCUS is a journey from one vision to the next, one process to the next. We cannot accomplish goals, tasks or reach milestones in our lives, without being focused. We must have tunnel vision to reach our destination at the appointed time.

'BLINK and FOCUS.'

Our eyes blink to make sure they stay focused on what they are viewing at that time. If our eyes are open, they receive information. Remember, blinking helps to remove the trash out of our eyes to stay focused. Blinking helps to lubricate the eyes, and to "refocus" on what we were viewing.

FOCUS KEY

There is a purpose to why we see what we see. When we see what we see, and what we do with what we see, is what makes the difference.

PAUSE

Write down what God just said or is saying right now in this chapter!

_____

_____

_____

_____

Stay focused and locked-in as you continue to read this book.

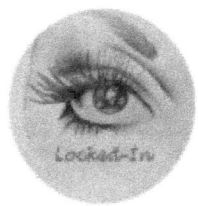

CHAPTER SIX

PITFALLS OF WANDERING

According to Merriam-Webster Dictionary, "wandering" means going about from place to place; movement away from the proper, normal, or usual course or place; characterized by aimless, slow, or pointless movement. Often, when we are "wandering" through life looking, we have our eyes on everything, but God. We tend to develop a "wandering" eye; looking at obstacles and circumstances that we see daily.

However, our eyes should be focused, not "wandering". God wants us to FOCUS on one thing, "HIM". Therefore, with the ability to see everything, we must first understand that God's purpose was for us, to keep our FOCUS on His Word.

But the men who had gone up with him said, "We are not able to go up against the people, or they are stronger than we." And they gave the children of Israel a bad report of the land which they had spied out, saying,

"The land through which we have gone as spies is a land that devours its inhabitants, and all the people whom we saw in it are men of great stature. There we saw the giants (the descendants of Anak came from the giants); and we were like grasshoppers in our own sight, and so we were in their sight." Then Caleb quieted the people before Moses, and said, "Let us go up at once and take possession, for we are well able to overcome it."

Numbers 13:30-33

Caleb said "Let us stay FOCUS on the Word of God, and not wander our FOCUS toward what was revealed." But the people lost heart and rebelled; refusing to enter Canaan. Instead, they cried for a new leader who would take them back to Egypt.

To punish them for their lack of faith, God condemned all that generation, except Caleb and Joshua, to perish in the wilderness for 40 years.

Num. 14:26-38

All those 20-years-old and up, would indeed perish in the wilderness, except for Joshua and Caleb.

When we allow issues and transactions that may occur before our very eyes, or things that does not necessarily apply to us, we tend to develop a "wandering "eye. When we allow ourselves to become "wanderers" in certain situations and times. Those can be troublesome times; especially in marriage and relationships. The "wandering" eye is the number one cause of getting us off FOCUS. When you 'wander' in conversations, especially those that you were not invited, it causes you to become defensive and offensive. The Word of God says take no offense.

"And blessed (happy, fortunate, and to be envied) is he who takes no offense at Me and finds no cause for stumbling in or through Me and is not hindered from seeing the Truth."

Matthew 11:6

'Wandering' can have negative influence and cause others to stumble. When you experience negative feelings about someone, you can find yourself "wandering". You begin to see or view, the way others want you to see about an individual, thing or situation. When that happens, you have allowed others to influence you. They could eventually change your beliefs and values.

O foolish Galatians! Who has bewitched you that you should not obey the truth, before whose eyes Jesus Christ was clearly portrayed among you as crucified?

Galatians 3:1

FOCUS KEY

Do not wander.
"FOCUS"

PAUSE

Write down what God just said or is saying right now in this chapter!

_____

_____

_____

_____

Stay focused and locked-in as you continue to read this book.

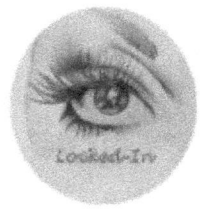

CHAPTER SEVEN
THE CATERPILLAR UNDERSTANDS FOCUS

God spoke to the caterpillar. He told him that he would receive wings to fly and germinate. The caterpillar looked at himself and said, "I do not see any wings."

While we do not look at the things which are seen, but at the things which are not seen. For the things, which are seen are temporary, but the things which are not seen are eternal.

2 Corinthians 4:18.

The caterpillar was focused on what God said to believe. He began his journey in becoming a butterfly. The transformation from caterpillar into a pupa (cocoon) is brought about in less than twenty hours. The familiar striped caterpillar has just ended its frantic eating spree. It determinedly leaves the leaves of the milkweed that have sustained it so far. This journey away may lead it to another milkweed, but usually to something totally different. Wherever it ends up, it will offer shelter from the scorching sun and the rain. When the caterpillar makes this junket, it is dogged in its search. Changes are already occurring anatomically that will continue to completion inexorably. If the caterpillar is not successful soon enough, the changes will immobilize it in vulnerable circumstances.

A butterfly metamorphosis requires four stages, the egg, larva, pupa, and the adult stage. During the egg stage, it is just a small oval or round egg, usually laid on leaves. After hatching, the larva stage or caterpillar takes place. The caterpillar grows instantly and very quickly when it starts to eat.

THE CATERPILLAR MUST FIND A SUITABLE SITE

It must attach himself in a timely manner, but usually to some place entirely safe and will offer shelter from the scorching sun and the rain, wind and storm. If the caterpillar is not successful soon enough, by reaching its destination, the changes will immobilize it in vulnerable circumstances. He does not have anything to do with his changing process or protection. It is all God.

THE CATERPILLAR UNDERSTOOD

The caterpillar understands that he must be moved by God's purpose and plan. The goal is to fly one day. He knows at this moment as a caterpillar, he does not physically have wings; nor does he visibly see wings. He knows that he will have wings at the end of this journey. His purpose is to fly. As a caterpillar, he knows one day he will fly. Finally, when all the changes are made, a butterfly will emerge. Once he becomes a butterfly, he cannot be transformed back to a caterpillar.

We must continue our journey of discovering who God said that we are, and we will understand that, when we FOCUS on His Word.

Therefore, if anyone is in Christ, he is a new creation; old things have passed away; behold, all things have become new.

2 Corinthians 5:17

FOCUS KEY

But they that wait upon the Lord shall renew their strength; they shall mount up with wings as eagles; they shall run, and not be weary, and they shall walk, and not faint.

Isaiah 40:31

PAUSE

Write down what God just said or is saying right now in this chapter!

_____

_____

_____

_____

Stay focused and locked-in as you continue to read this book.

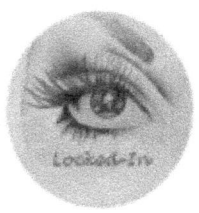

CHAPTER EIGHT
FOCUS ON THE BODY

FOCUS on the body is like walking alone with Jesus. The disciples walked with Him, while capturing the presence of Jesus. We must continue to walk with Him now in the spirit. FOCUS always has an awareness of the very presence of Jesus. The spirit of Him should surrounds and captivates our being.

It was interesting how Jesus walked with two of the disciples on the road to Emmaus. Yet, they could not recognize Him supernaturally. However, Jesus was there all the time in the natural. Every believer of Christ can experience the presence of Jesus. We have the Holy Spirit, that is on the inside of us.

And they talked together of all these things which had happened. So it was, while they conversed and reasoned that Jesus Himself drew near and went with them. But their eyes were restrained, so that they did not know Him.

> Luke 24:14-16

We know Him and our eyes are not restrained. We can now understand the value of FOCUS as it is revealed. FOCUS is being: **F**ull **O**f **C**onsistent **U**nlimited **S**ight in the things of God. Therefore, not just revealing Himself, Jesus chose to walk with them, and share scriptures about Him. Jesus is always speaking, but we must always have an ear to hear what the Spirit is saying to us.

    For example, picture walking side by side with Jesus as He taught, but not knowing it was Christ Himself. What an awesome experience it would be for you and I! The disciples started their journey wondering about what had happened, and ended up walking with Him! Focusing on the body is like walking alone with Jesus as the disciples did in the natural; while capturing the presence of Jesus, as we continue to walk with Him now, in the spirit. FOCUS always has an awareness of the very presence of Jesus, as the Spirit of Him surrounds and captivates our being.

    I can recall the time when I was on a convoy in Iraq. I saw a shepherd walking down the road with a herd of sheep following Him. The shepherd walked at such a moderate pace with such authority and grace. While the sheep were quite the opposite, stumbling over one another, speeding up and slowing down. Yet, they were fully aware that they would not get ahead of the shepherd. This could describe sheep in the church. Sheep in the church today are stumbling over one another. They speed up and slow down, but fully aware that they should not get ahead of the shepherd. FOCUS will keep us following, but distractions will cause us to stray, and get out of position.

I continued looking and focusing on the shepherd, as he journeyed down the road. At that very moment, I saw a vision of myself leading people. God revealed to me that I was that shepherd. The people would be following me stumbling, confused, weary, but content. They would have the assurance that they are going the right way, and that their FOCUS was not to get ahead, but to follow. This was my visitation and call to pastor. God was there all along walking with me. True FOCUS is staying in place knowing that God will never leave nor forsake us.

May the LORD our God be with us, as He was with our fathers. May He not leave us nor forsake us.

1 Kings 8:57

DEFEATING THE DEVIL

Why FOCUS on the body? If we neglect the very thing that God has given the church for battle to defeat Satan, we will not survive. We will become injured, wounded, weak, weary and sick trying to survive.

But God said, "Greater is He (Holy Spirit) that is in us than he that is in the world."

1 John 4:4

When we are equipped with a lethal weapon, we can launch an attack that will demolish and destroy the wiles of the devil.

The thief does not come except to steal, and to kill, and to destroy. I have come that they may have life and that they may have it more abundantly.

John 10:10

Abundant life comes with our FOCUS on the body of Christ. Focusing covers our natural body and brings fulfillment through God's plan for our life. When our body is covered, we become more aware of what's happening and what may be coming in our future. We can figure out what will happen; although we may not figure out, when it will happen. However, it is not important to FOCUS on when, we want to FOCUS on what. If we're right about what, we don't have to worry about when.

I wonder sometimes, how is it that the church has gotten away from the very thing that God has given us to defeat Satan? How have we become so distracted? My answer is, we took our FOCUS off the body of Christ, therefore leaving our body uncovered. Jesus cautioned the disciples not to be distracted. When we FOCUS on Christ, others can FOCUS on our body.

You are our epistle written in our hearts, known and read by all men.

2 Corinthians 3:2

Much of the church is moved more by what they see, rather than, what the Gospel has said, "Cover your body with the Word."

Now it happened as they journeyed on the road, someone said to Him, "Lord, I will follow You wherever You go." And Jesus said to him, "Foxes have holes and birds of the air have nests, but the Son of Man has nowhere to lay His head." Then He said to another, "Follow Me." But he said, "Lord, let me first go and bury my father." Jesus said to him, "Let the dead bury their own dead, but you go and preach the kingdom of God." And another also said, "Lord I will follow You, but let me first go and bid them farewell who are at my house." But Jesus said to him, "No one, having put his hand to the plow, and looking back, is fit for the kingdom of God."

Luke 9:57-62

What was Jesus saying at that very moment? In so many words he was saying. "Not now disciples. Let's stay focused on the plan that our Father has given us to carry out. Since we cannot see all the way down the road, at least we can stay focused on Him." It is extremely important that we cannot allow our current situation to distract us from a permanent situation. The bible reminds us that we are seated in heavenly places with God. Allowing distractions of this world will cause our destiny, that is full of blessing, be aborted. Therefore, we cannot fulfill the plan that God has for you and I.

Do you know that God uses pastors to "disciple" his people; and they can lead the sheep through their journey? Success comes from our FOCUS on our pastor's directions and instructions.

WHEN WE FOCUS ON THE BODY OF CHRIST, WE WILL SEE ORDER

God is a God of Order. We must be careful we do not become double minded and unstable. We can profit from some of the trials that we go through. The bible is clear in saying,

"My brethren, count it all joy when you fall into various trials, knowing that the testing of your faith produces patience. But let patience have its perfect work, that you may be perfect and complete, lacking nothing. If any of you lacks wisdom, let him ask of God, who gives to all liberally and without reproach, and it will be given to him. But let him ask in faith, with no doubting, for he who doubts is like a wave of the sea driven and tossed by the wind. For let not that man supposes that he will receive anything from the Lord; he is a double-minded man, unstable in all his ways."

James 1:2-8

It is dishonorable and double minded trying to have two heads. It brings disorder, and it is dysfunctional when putting anything in front of God. Can you imagine, Jesus is telling the disciples to follow Him. Instead, we walk away, and ask someone else should they go? The same analogy applies with your pastor. He is God's
delegated authority. When you do not follow your pastor's lead, which brings order, it causes division. It causes us to be tossed to and fro.

"We should no longer be children, tossed to and fro and carried about with every wind of doctrine, by the trickery of men, in the cunning craftiness of deceitful plotting."

Ephesians 4:14

Did you know that when you resist sound council from your pastor, you are breaking protocol and resisting God?

As we continue our journey, we must stay focused. Let us not look at what has happened in the past. So far, we have received divine revelation of the value of FOCUS. Focusing on the body is checking your body to ensure that everything is in place. It is making certain that every part is functioning and ready for battle. This is called a Preventive Maintenance Check or PMCS.

PREVENTIVE MAINTENANCE CHECK AND SERVICES (PMCS)

A soldier will not go into battle without doing a PMCS on themselves and his or her equipment. The church has entered battle without counting the cost. The church accepted Christ without reading the instructions, or the fine print. It states that to be a successful soldier, in the army of God, we must first FOCUS on the Body of Christ. This ensures that our body is covered before trying to deal with Satan and his army. In those instructions, it states that to fulfill the promises of God, we must be equipped for battle. We must first be renewed in the spirit of our mind.

"Therefore, I urge you, brethren, by the mercies of God, to present your bodies a living and holy sacrifice, acceptable to

God, which is your spiritual service of worship. And do not be conformed to this world, but be transformed by the renewing of your mind, so that you may prove what the will of God is, that which is good and acceptable and perfect."

Romans 12:1-2

Then, John says;
But the hour is coming, and now is, when the true worshipers will worship the Father in spirit and truth; for the Father is seeking such to worship Him. God is Spirit, and those who worship Him must worship in spirit and truth.

John 4:23-24

If our mind is not renewed by the Word of God, we may not be ready for battle. That is called battle fatigue. We will fight in the natural, or in our flesh, rather than engaging in spiritual warfare.

For we are not fighting against flesh and blood enemies, but against evil rulers and authorities of the unseen world, against mighty powers in this dark world, and against evil spirits in the heavenly places.

Ephesians 6:12

COVERING YOUR BODY IS TO FOCUS ON YOUR ARMOR

Paul told the Ephesians church to FOCUS on their bodies and cover it up. We see the Apostle Paul, and how he exhorts and directs the church in Ephesus. He teaches them how to behave themselves in spiritual warfare, by combatting the enemies of their soul and mind. He proposes the idea of spiritual armor, and how important it is to preserve and defend them in the conflict. When launching your attack, never go to battle without your armor. That's your protection. FOCUS on putting on the whole armor of God.

Finally, my brethren, be strong in the Lord and in the power of His might. Put on the whole armor of God that you may be able to stand against the wiles of the devil. For we do not wrestle against flesh and blood, but against principalities, against powers, against the rulers of the darkness of this age, against spiritual hosts of wickedness in the heavenly places. Therefore, take up the whole armor of God that you may be able to withstand in the evil day, and having done all, to stand. Stand therefore, having girded your waist with truth; and having on the breastplate of righteousness.

Ephesians 6:10-14

Our FOCUS should be standing, and allowing truth to be the foundation of a covered body. The first thing Paul is telling the body of Christ is to stand. In other words, he is demanding that we get FOCUS.

The U.S. Army has General Orders. The First General Order, says, "I will guard everything within the limits of my post and quit my post, only when properly relieved." This is accomplished by, keeping my ground, and not deserting my post. This order applies also to the body of Christ. It means keeping your ground and not deserting your call, responsibilities and duties. It means not becoming uncovered, and continuing your journey by finishing your work, as you stand guard. Spouses stand with one another, the body of Christ stands with one another, by way of our local churches. Children stand with their parents.

Honor your father and mother, which is the first commandment with promise.

Ephesians 6:20

Let the Word of Christ dwell in you richly in all wisdom, teaching and admonishing one another in psalms and hymns and spiritual songs, singing with grace in your hearts to the Lord.

Colossians 3:16

Transformation takes place in our standing. Why? Because if we don't stand for something, we will fall for anything.

- Standing on what truth is in our lives and the righteousness of God, and by allowing righteousness to operate in our lives.
- Standing is staying FOCUS.

    I will stand my watch and set myself on the rampart, and watch to see what He will say to me, and what I will answer when I am corrected.

    Habakkuk 2:1

When we are standing, we are under His authority. When we are not standing, we are falling away from His authority. Once we begin to FOCUS and take responsibility of our position, then we can begin to tie everything together with truth. We are prepared for spiritual battle, first in the natural, then in the spirit. Battle is about strategy. We cannot allow the enemy to get us distracted, placing us in a depressed state. This will cause us to be paralyze on the battle field. Focusing on truth determines our level of victory in battle.

Having girded your waist with truth.

Ephesians 6:14

Our foundation and victory begins with walking in truth. You also were included in Christ when you heard the Word of truth, the Gospel of your salvation.

Having believed, you were marked in Him with a seal, the promised Holy Spirit.

Ephesians 1:13

WHAT IS TRUTH?

That
Reality
Underneath
The
Heart

God deals with our heart and He wants to deal with what is real. Real is that reality from our heart.

Then Jesus said, "And you shall know the truth, and the truth shall make you free."

John 8:32

Society and the church can survive on **T**hat **R**eality **U**nderneath **T**he **H**eart. We are to be genuine (real) with one another; our spouse, our children, our employer and neighbors, because this is the heart of God. We should never operate away from the truth. Truth stands, and a lie crumbles.

The Word of God says,
"You are of your father the devil, and it is your will to practice the desires [which are characteristics] of your father. He was a murderer from the beginning, and does not stand in the truth because there is no truth in him. When he lies, he speaks what it changes to is natural to him, for he is a liar and the father of lies and half-truths."

John 8:44

When there is truth, there is support, meaning we are "all in." We are sold out. Our mind is made up that we believe in God, and that we are fighting the right battle for the cause of winning souls for the kingdom. Therefore, I obey his instructions and guidance through the delegated authority. When our loins are girt with truth, we do not depart from the truth. Truth strengthens us against the assaults and attacks of Satan. It is of great use in our spiritual conflict with the enemy.

Our righteousness should be the girdle of our loins and faithfulness the girdle of our reins with Christ.

Isaiah 11:5

God desires truth, that is, sincerity, in the inward parts.

Psalms 51:6

This is the strength of our loins; and it girds on all other pieces of our armor, and therefore is first mentioned. If we do not allow truth to pull us in, we find ourselves fighting a lie and dealing with distractions. The purpose of a girdle is to pull the body in. Just as truth girds and holds all the pieces of armor, truth holds the family, society, and the church and covers it. Once we begin to FOCUS and take responsibility of our position, then we can begin to tie everything together and prepare for a spiritual battle—and we can win when we FOCUS on the body of Christ so that we remain covered!

FOCUS KEY

Once we begin to FOCUS. We take responsibility of our position. Then we can begin to tie everything together and prepare for a spiritual battle. We can win when we FOCUS on the body of Christ so that we remain covered!

PAUSE

Write down what God just said or is saying right now in this chapter!

_____

_____

_____

_____

Stay focused and locked-in as you continue to read this book.

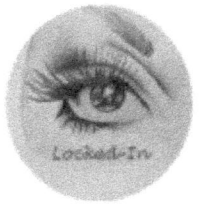

CHAPTER NINE
TOUGH NATURALLY VS TOFF SPIRITUALLY

TOFF is standing in **T**ruth of that Reality Underneath **T**he **H**eart. **O**rder keeps us walking by **F**aith, while allowing **FOCUS** to become the key to the more abundant life. The acronyms for TOFF is...

Truth
Order
Faith
Focus

In this season, it has been very difficult to FOCUS on the Word of God. There is a beast in the land that is causing many distractions. The beast is Social Media. Through various means of media, powers orchestrated by the enemy. Its mission is to seek, deceive, deprive and destroy the authority that the church has.

Social Media has become the dragon that blows fire upon us that makes it difficult to escape. It has such a tremendous stronghold on society. Wall Street, Main Street and the church are running around with their heads down. They are like chickens pecking for more and more. Who dare not to depart from their cell phones? It is time to mount up, hold your head up and FOCUS. God promises in His Word,

"They that wait on the LORD shall renew their strength; they shall mount up with wings like eagles, they shall run and not be weary, they shall walk (focus) and not faint.

Isaiah 40:31

Cell phones have begun to crawl over and distract fellowship at the dinner table, on the job, crossing the street and shopping. People even text while driving.

The thief does not come except to steal, and to kill, and to destroy. I have come that they may have life and that they may have it more abundantly.

John 10:10

Society and the body of believers are experiencing fire from the dragon that is being distracted like never in this season.

For whatever is born of God overcomes the world. And this is the victory that has overcome the world—our faith.

1 John 5:4

"And I saw something like a sea of glass mingled with fire, and those who have the victory over the beast, over his image and over his mark and over the number of his name, standing on the sea of glass, having harps of God."

Revelation 15:2

Thank God that He has given us the solution in dealing with issues! God said to me in 2014, There is a Call in the Land to FOCUS Because Society is Caught in a Web of Distraction. He is saying it is time to get tough (a violent aggressive person) not in the natural, but TOFF by the spirit using the principles of the Word of God as our sword. Jesus is clear when he says,

"For the Father loves the Son, and shows Him all things that He Himself does; and He will show Him greater works than these, that you may marvel."

John 5:20

TOFF is standing in **T**ruth, having **O**rder, walking by **F**aith, and staying **F**ocused. We are the New Generational Church on the Rise. What that means is having a focused mind set, not a new church. A "FOCUS" mind-set understands the signs of the time.

The sons of Issachar who understood the times, to know what Israel ought to do.

> 1 Chronicles 12:32

The sons of Issachar knew what Israel ought to do. Should we, the sons of God, know what society ought to do in this season? The sons of God are the New Generational Church, on the Rise. We are TOFF in spirit, not tough in the natural.

The dictionary gives meaning of the word, "TOFF", as a stylishly dressed, fashionable person; especially one who is or wants to be considered a member of the upper class. It is nob or an informal term for an upper-class or wealthy person. Basically, according to the American Heritage Dictionary, the definition of nob means, a rich or a man who is wealthy. TOFF is a British Slang.

"You are of God, little children, and have overcome them, because He who is in you is greater than he who is in the world."

> 1 John 4:4

For we are rich and wealthy in Christ. On the other hand, being TOFF in God is four foundational truths. These truths will be our transition to success as the New Generational

Church, on the Rise. It will ensure the more abundant life by eliminating the dragon distractions. New Generational mindset has become the period of time. It is when we become focused more in the Word of God, and not distracted by the cares of this world. New Generational mindsets are empowered to accept that we must fulfill our commission to go and make disciples.

There is a cleansing coming in this season, as we transition into the Word of God. Don't feel discouraged, sad or blue. We are going into something new. Stay determined and steadfast, while moving toward becoming a New Generational Church on the Rise, with a renewed mindset. It is time to fight!

"Fight the good fight of faith, lay hold on eternal life, to which you were also called and have confessed the good confession in the presence of many witnesses"

1 Timothy 6:12

The worst thing that could happen to someone, is for them to find themselves in a fight when they don't even know how to fight. We are going to learn how to fight and win.

For we have been crucified with Christ; "It is no longer I who live, but Christ lives in me; and the life which I now live in the flesh I live by faith in the Son of God, who loved me and gave Himself for me."

Galatians 2:20

So, he answered and said to me: This is the Word of the LORD to Zerubbabel, saying 'Not by might nor by power, but by My Spirit,' says the LORD of hosts.

Zechariah 4:6

Finally, it is time to blow the dragon out the water by the Spirit of the Word of God. 'I say then:

"Walk in the Spirit, and you shall not fulfill the lust of the flesh. For the flesh lusts against the Spirit and the Spirit against the flesh; and these are contrary to one another, so that you do not do the things that you wish. But if you are led by the Spirit, you are not under the law."

Galatians 5:16-17

Let's get TOFF!

TOFF is fighting with the understanding of four words. If received and carried out, there is no way we cannot defeat the tricks and schemes of the devil.

"But be ye doers of the word, and not hearers only, deceiving your own selves."

James 1:22

TOFF
TRUTH, ORDER,
FAITH AND FOCUS

TRUTH
That **R**eality **U**nderneath, **T**he **H**eart,

And you shall know the truth, and the truth shall make you free."

John 8:32

God deals with **T**ruth that comes from **T**he **H**eart. Marriages stand on **T**ruth; relationships stand and are built on **T**ruth. We raise our children to tell the **T**ruth. Our children want us to be truthful, and our employer expects **T**ruth. The **R**eality of **T**ruth comes from our **H**eart that the sender and recipient, God desires.

Behold, you desire truth in the innermost being, and in the hidden part (of my heart). You will make me know wisdom.

Psalms 51:6

Only fear the LORD and serve Him in truth with all your heart; for consider what great things He has done for you.

1 Sam 12:24

The LORD may continue His Word which He spoke concerning me, saying, "If thy children take heed to their way, to walk before me in truth with all their heart and with all their soul, there shall not fail thee (said he) a man on the throne of Israel."

1 Kings 2:4

Then the woman said to Elijah, "Now by this I know that you are a man of God, and that the Word of the LORD in your mouth is the truth."

1 Kings 17:24

When we walk, and operate in the spirit of truth, people will trust, believe and work for you.

ORDER

Walking in **O**bedience and being in **R**ight Standing with God, that causes a **D**ecision to be made that will be **E**ffective in its **Re**lease. God is a God of **Order,**

Let all things be done decently and in order.

1 Corinthians 14:40

    Remember being TOFF is **Order**. We want to be over comers, but it starts with our **O**bedience in what God has said to us. Through **O**bedience, we place ourselves in **R**ight **S**tanding with Him. In life, there is always **D**ecisions that need to be made. If you want to get in your car and go to the other side, you must first decide to open the door and place the key into the ignition and turn it to crank the car.

God took the man and set him down in the Garden of Eden to work the ground and keep it in order.

Genesis 2:15

However, something happened when man was not in **O**rder. His disobedience and not being in **R**ight **S**tanding with God, that when man had to decide, it was not **E**ffective in its **R**elease in the earth. Therefore, humanity suffered. Whenever there is a **D**ecision to be made, we must follow Gods **O**rder of **O**bedience. Staying in **R**ight **S**tanding with Him is key. When **D**ecision time comes, it must be **E**ffective in its **R**elease in the earth. When we operate in the spirit of **O**rder, people will trust, believe, work for you and with you.

FAITH

Faith is having **F**ull **A**ccess **I**nto **T**he **H**eavens.

Now faith is the substance of things hoped for, the evidence of things not seen. For by it the elders obtained a good testimony. By faith we understand that the worlds were framed by the Word of God, so that the things which are seen were not made of things which are visible.

Hebrews 11:1-3

But without faith it is impossible to please Him, for he who comes to God must believe that He is, and that He is a rewarder of those who diligently seek Him.

Hebrews 11:6

Therefore, when we walk by faith and not by sight, the reward is that we are given "**F**ull **A**ccess **I**nto **T**he **H**eavens" because of our faith. Satan is less concerned about your body. He attacks our faith to attempt to cause doubt and unbelief to come forth. There is no truth in Satan, for "you are the children of your father the devil, and you love to do the evil things he does. He was a murderer from the beginning. He has always hated the truth, because there is no truth in him. When he lies, it is consistent with his character;

"For he is a liar and the father of lies."

John 8:44

When you operate in the spirit of faith, people will trust, believe and work for you, and with you.

FOCUS

FOCUS is **F**ull **O**f **C**onsistent **U**nlimited **S**ight in the Word of God. Focus is the key to the more abundant life. Jesus was so focused on the Word of God, He stayed consistent with **U**nlimited **S**ight in His Words.

Being FOCUS is not just another gospel. It is a call in the land by God to FOCUS; because society is caught in a web of distraction. FOCUS goes into another level of thinking and makes things happen. Jesus is saying I am fed up with

the distraction and I am going to do something about it.

"If my people, which are called by my name, shall humble themselves, and pray, and seek my face, and turn from their wicked ways; then will I hear from heaven, and will forgive their sin, and will heal their land."
2 Chronicles 7:14

Look back on your life and identify the things that were accomplished. You can contribute the victory to your FOCUS. However, when we look back on what we did not accomplish it is mainly because the enemy caused use to become distracted. It is amazing that God has given us everything that pertains to life and godliness. He has created a plan for our lives. Yet, we have allowed distraction to destroy our destiny in Christ by being unfocused.

Accept the call to FOCUS and eliminate the distractions. With the confession of our mouth and believing in our heart we are no longer distracted.

Therefore, my beloved brethren, be steadfast (focus), immovable, always abounding in the work of the Lord, knowing that your labor is not in vain in the Lord.

> 1 Corinthians 15:58

FOCUS is the mind of God. It is the plan of God, and the decisions of God. God is interested in change, in the church and in society. His desire is for believers to become holy and set apart. He does not only desire us to read what He said, but doing what He says. No longer will the church be described as;

Having a form of Godliness but denying the power thereof.

> 2 Timothy 3:5

But know this: in the last day's perilous times will come, but we are not going to be partakers because we have raised our level of FOCUS.

FOCUS FUNCTION IS IN TRUST, FAITH AND FOCUS

We are going to discover how trust, faith and FOCUS function together. There is a difference between trust, faith and FOCUS. However, there is also a correlation (relation) between trust, faith and FOCUS. I submit to you that trust, faith and FOCUS need one another. They go hand and hand.

   The key to having healthy relationships, lies in staying focused with one another. We must trust one another and have faith in one another. Maintaining relationships can be difficult. Some may not stand. This is true in business and partnerships also. We must trust and have faith.

   It is equally important to stay focused on what we are doing, while staying current with the signs of the times. FOCUS sees faith working and stands with trust. By faith we receive our healing, while focusing on the process and trusting His Word.

The Word of the Lord is right; and all his works are done in truth.
Psalms 33:4

I can trust Jeremiah when He says,

For I will restore health unto you, and I will heal you of your wounds as I FOCUS on what He said."

Jeremiah 30:17

I can believe, by faith, in what Isaiah says,

"But he was wounded for our transgressions, he was bruised for our iniquities: the chastisement of our peace was upon him; and with his stripes we are healed,"

Isaiah 53:5

I can FOCUS on Isaiah when He says,

But they that wait upon the Lord shall renew their strength; they shall mount up with wings as eagles; they shall run, and not be weary, and they shall walk and not faint,"

Isaiah 40:31

FOCUS is that **U**nlimited **S**ight that we operate in as we are **C**onsistent in **T**rust, **C**onsistent in our **F**aith and **C**onsistent in our FOCUS on His Word. That goes hand and hand. They work together. They talk and walk together. Let us go over to the other side, and continue to discover how trust, faith and FOCUS function together.

Trust in the Lord with all thine heart; and lean not unto thine own understanding. In all thy ways acknowledge him, and he shall direct thy paths.

Proverbs 3:5-6

Without faith, it is impossible to please him: He that cometh to God must believe that He is, and that he is a re-warder of them that diligently seek him.

Hebrews 11:6

Therefore, we must diligently FOCUS on Him to receive our reward.

Now faith (now FOCUS) is the substance of things hoped for (your focus is your hope), the evidence of things not seen.

Hebrews 11:1

Substance is defined as material possessions, goods and wealth. It is a person of substance; that of which a thing consists. Substance is a physical matter or material or form. In biology, substance becomes and activates any agency bringing about activation. It is a molecule that increases the activity of an enzyme or a protein that increases the production of a gene product in DNA transcription. Activator may refer to: Activator (genetics); a DNA-binding protein that regulates one or more genes by increasing the rate of transcription Activator.

FOCUS is that molecule that increases the activity of our faith. It increases the production of the spirit of Jesus in His DNA transcription. This is the first step of gene expression. FOCUS is the substance. It increases our level of faith because we have **U**nlimited **S**ight. That means, we will not waver or doubt. We will not lose our FOCUS on what the Word of God says. When He says, "Trust", we will. When He says, "Believe", we will. When He says, "Have faith", we will, and when He says, "FOCUS", we can.

"But seek (FOCUS) ye first the kingdom of God, and his righteousness; and all these things shall be added unto you."

Matthew 6:33

"And I say unto you, Ask, and it shall be given you; seek (FOCUS), and ye shall find; knock, and it shall be opened unto you"

Luke 11:9

STAY TOFF AND STAY FOCUSED

FOCUS KEY

FOCUS is that molecule that increases the activity of our faith. It increases the production of the spirit of Jesus in His DNA transcription. It is the first step of gene expression. Therefore, standing TOFF is fighting supernaturally!

PAUSE

Write down what God just said or is saying right now in this chapter!

_____

_____

_____

_____

Stay focused and locked-in as you continue to read this book.

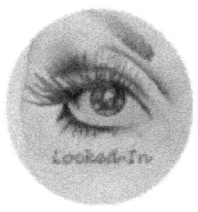

CHAPTER TEN
IT IS TIME TO SHIFT OUR FOCUS

It is time to shift. It is time for a revolution. Shifting and revolution brings a fundamental change in power. This is the power that the church can operate by. This is the season of shifting our FOCUS back to the Word of God. It is eliminating the distraction of the world, and its views of how we should function as the body of Christ.

There is a paradigm shift taking place. It is a revolutionary change from one way of thinking to another. It is a transformation or metamorphosis, rather than an evolutionary process. The paradigm we chose, accept, and use. It depends on the church believing, what we perceive to be true and accurate.

God called Abram before he was Abraham. His orders to him was to leave his country and to get away from family and friends. Abram trusted God enough to change his way of thinking. His trust was based on his relationships. He simply obeyed God's command.

Now the LORD had said to Abram: "Get out of your country, from your family and from your father's house, to a land that I will show you. I will make you a great nation; I will bless you and make your name great; and you shall be a blessing. I will bless those who bless you, and I will curse him who curses you; and in you all the families of the earth shall be blessed."

Genesis 12:1-5

Keep in mind, Abram's father Terah was a wicked idolatrous priest who manufactured idols. Abram, in opposition to his father's idol shop, smashed his father's idols and chased customers away. God is trying to take us away from a lot of places we are unwilling to go.

"If we are willing and obedient we shall eat the good of the land."

Isaiah 1:19

God promised to make Abraham's name great. This promise hold true for us too. The only way God can make our name great that we shall be a blessing, but it only comes through our obedience. If we are not experiencing the blessing, could it be because of our disobedience? Abram was obedient and followed God. The question for you and I would be, "Will you follow

Him?" He is asking all the time, "Will you go?" Can you hear Him beckoning you to make a shift? It is time to shift!

SHIFT MEANS TO:
S=Separate from
H=Habits and
I=Influence
F=For
T=Transformation

When we talk about shifting our FOCUS, we should be at the point of finally **S**eparating from negative **H**abits and **I**nfluence **F**or **T**ransformation. This shifting will elevate the call that God made to you to become FOCUS; which means to be **F**ull **O**f **C**onsistent and **U**nlimited **S**ight in the Word of God. Jesus was so consistent He only did what His Father told Him to do.

Shifting our FOCUS moves the believer from one place to another. It removes us from not knowing, to a place of knowing. It transcends us from a place of darkness to light. It moves us from thinking negative, to a place of thinking positive. Lastly, it elevates us from a place of defeat, to a place of victory. Shifting our FOCUS means to **S**eparate from negative **H**abits and **I**nfluences. It is key to your **T**ransformation into the man and women God created you and I to be.

It is amazing in the beginning how God saw that separation was needed. He created the light that was God, darkness is also lurking. This is true in relationships and situations. Therefore, we must begin to hear what our spirit is saying unto us. God commands separation. When the body of Christ begins to FOCUS and **S**eparate from darkness, as God saw. The light is good, but separation may be needed.

God saw that the light was good (pleasing, useful) and He affirmed and sustained it. God separated the light [distinguishing it] from the darkness.

Genesis 1:4

When we allow separation to take place through relationships; God will reveal His purpose and plan that He has for our lives.

And the Lord said to Abram, after Lot had separated from him: "Lift your eyes now and look from the place where you are—northward, southward, eastward, and westward."

Genesis 13:14

God did not reveal His plan to Abram until he was separated from Lot. God is saying, "There is a call in the land to FOCUS because society and the church is caught in a Web of Distraction. We should understand that whether in the church or society, we are all God's people. His instructions were to bring an awareness to His people to FOCUS on His WORD. We must recognize and not get caught up in distractions.

"So it will be at the end of the age. "The angels will come forth, separate the wicked from among the just."

Matthew 13:49

"All the nations will be gathered before Him, and He will separate them one from another, as a shepherd divides his sheep from the goats."

Matthew 25:32

SHIFT AND SEPARATE FROM UNWANTED HABITS

We must begin to **S**eparate from words that are not of God. If we do not, words that are received, can become **H**abits that is not pleasing to God. Negative **H**abits that have become like second nature to us, does not belong to us. They are unwanted attachments that have disguised itself as the angel of light. They are carriers of darkness. Some attachment sounds something like, 'This is just the way I am'. **H**abits that have attached themselves becomes oblivious. Some, we are not aware of, or not concerned about. Many are happenings around us that we have gotten used to. We never fully see or recognize, the position that Satan has placed us in.

Therefore, if we do not **S**eparate from those unwanted **H**abits, they can become our character that will ultimately lead to our destiny.

"But if we walk in the light as He is in the light, we have fellowship with one another, and the blood of Jesus Christ His Son cleanses us from all sin."

1 John 1:7

A quote from Frank Outlaw was published in a Texas newspaper feature called "What They're Saying" in May 1977. The saying was ascribed to the creator of a successful U.S. supermarket chain called Bi-Lo that says: "Watch your thoughts, they become words; watch your words, they become actions; watch your actions, they become habits; watch your habits, they become character; watch your character, for it becomes your destiny." If we know that our **H**abits do not define who we are in Christ, **S**eparate from that which is defining you! **S**eparate right now, and **S**hift your FOCUS.

If my people who are called by My name will humble themselves, and pray and seek My face, and turn from their wicked ways, then I will hear from heaven, and will forgive their sin and heal their land.

2 Chronicles 7:14

SEPARATE AND DEPART FROM NEGATIVE HABITS AND INFLUENCE FOR TRANSFORMATION

Shift and **S**eparate from Negative **I**nfluence. **I**nfluence is the power that somebody must affect other people's thinking or actions by means of argument, example, force of personality or intimidation. People can become intimidated based on how you look at them. On the other hand, you can be intimated by how a person may look at you. Some people purposely positions themselves, because they look to intimidate and **I**nfluence the outcome. They use this as a manipulation in expressing their views upon someone to **I**nfluence the outcome.

Then to Adam He said, "Because you have listened to the voice of your wife, and have eaten from the tree about which I commanded you, saying, 'You shall not eat from it'; Cursed is the ground because of you; In toil, you will eat of it All the days of your life."

Genesis 3:17-19

FOCUS overcomes **I**nfluence and **S**hifts our way of thinking to what God has said to us. Therefore, when we **S**hift our FOCUS it creates a whole new way of thinking. We begin to think the way God thinks, and see the way God sees.

My son, keep my words and treasure my commandments within you. Keep my commandments and live, and my teaching as the apple of your eye. Bind them on your fingers; Write them on the tablet of your heart. Say to wisdom, "You are my sister," And call understanding your intimate friend; that they may keep you from an adulteress, from the foreigner who flatters with her words.

Proverbs 7:1-5

One of the greatest influencer is someone that you care about, love and cherish with all your heart, soul and mind. I love my spouse, family and friends. Our love for God should be the ultimate, and the most influential person in our life. Therefore, when we are surrounded by negative **I**nfluence, rely on who is on the inside of you, the Holy Spirit. **S**hift your FOCUS to the Word of God, and the plan that God has promised for your life.

SHIFT OUR FOCUS FOR TRANSFORMATION

Transformation is making a complete change; usually into something with an improved appearance or usefulness. It is time for **T**ransformation into the New Man.

This I say, therefore, and testify in the Lord, "That you should no longer walk as the rest of the Gentiles walk, in the futility of their mind having their understanding darkened, being alienated from the life of God, because of the ignorance that is in them, because of the blindness of their heart; who, being past feeling, have given themselves over to lewdness, to work all uncleanness with greediness.

But you have not so learned Christ, if indeed you have heard Him and have been taught by Him, as the truth is in Jesus: that you put off, concerning your former conduct, the old man which grows corrupt according to the deceitful lusts, and be renewed in the spirit of your mind, and that you put on the new man which was created according to God, in true righteousness and holiness."

Ephesians 4:17-24

God wants the body of Christ to change their behavior in how they present themselves as the body of Christ.

I beseech you therefore, brethren, by the mercies of God, that you present your bodies a living sacrifice, holy, acceptable to God, which is your reasonable service.

And do not be conformed to this world, but be transformed by the renewing of your mind, that you may prove what is that good and acceptable and perfect will of God.
Romans 12:1-2

The sure way to prove what is that good and acceptable and perfect will of God would be to **S**hift and **FOCUS**.

FOCUS KEY

FOCUS overcomes the power of **N**egative **I**nfluence and **S**hifts our way of thinking to what God has said to us. It is time to **S**hift into God's rest for total transformation.

PAUSE

Write down what God just said or is saying right now in this chapter!

_____

_____

_____

_____

Stay focused and locked-in as you continue to read this book.

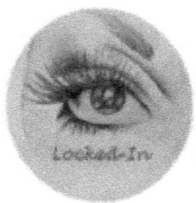

CONCLUSION

There Is a Call in the Land to FOCUS Because Society is Caught in a Web of Distraction. We entered the world of FOCUS through this book. The church and society is full of distractions. Many of the distractions have taken God's people and society off FOCUS from God and His Word.

This book was written to share the revelation given to me. My hope is to encourage, empower and guide you. We explored and identified the many traps and distractions in the church and society. We discovered many empowering FOCUS keys, and gave you step by step instructions on how to get TOFF and make your Shift. Ultimately, our main goal is to help you stay focused and locked-in your journey!

I pray that this book has encouraged you and given the ammunition needed to answer God's call on your life. Stay FOCUS and finish God's work. Read and study it repeatedly. "There Is a Call in The Land to FOCUS Because Society is Caught in a Web of Distractions" will help you finish the work,

So that your eager willingness to do it, may be matched by your completion of it, according to your means.

2 Corinthians 8:11

GET TOFF, SHIFT AND FOCUS

FOCUS KEYS

Stay FOCUS, make the SHIFT into God's Rest!

PAUSE

Write down what God just said or is saying right now in the CONCLUSION!

_____

_____

_____

_____

**YOU stayed focused and locked-in
You FINISHED reading this book!**

LET'S KEEP IN TOUCH

For more information about the ministry of Apostle Melvin E. Moore, and a list of available CD messages, books, publications, speaking engagements and spiritual growth and development resources, you may contact…

Kingdom Connection Christian Center International
Fayetteville, North Carolina

Email: mm1moore@aol.com

Website: kingdomconnectionministry.org

COMING SOON:

The Music CD: (CR) Call and Response to FOCUS

ABOUT THE AUTHOR

Apostle Melvin E. Moore

Apostle Melvin E. Moore was raised in Memphis, Tennessee by his parents, Will and Dorothy Moore. As he grew from childhood to manhood, God began to develop his love, his compassion and his mercy for people. God was preparing him for ministry.

His ministry was cultivated through God's rigorous training, diverse mentoring relationships and military chaplaincy programs. He served twenty-two years' in the military and served as an officer. His tours included Desert Storm, Desert Shield and Iraq.

He has been awarded outstanding awards and recognition for his excellence in leadership and managerial abilities. His educational achievements were received through several prominent colleges.

Apostle Melvin E. Moore is true to his covenant in marriage of 44 years to wife, Dr. Margaret H. Moore. They are blessed with three daughters, five grandchildren and two great-grandchildren.

He is founder of one of the fastest growing ministries, Kingdom Connection Christian Center International, Fayetteville North Carolina.

References/Credits

Strong J., Strong's Concordance (Popular Edition of the Exhaustive Concordance, *Thomas Nelson Publishers*

King James Bible, Early Modern English, 2011 Bible

Merriam-Webster's Dictionary (11th ed),(2005) Springfield, MA:

Outlaw, Frank (1977, May 18), "What They're Saying" Quote, San Antonio Light, p. 28, column 4

Zondervan NIV Study Bible General Editor, Kenneth L. Barker, full rev. ed., Zondervan, 2002

The English Standard Version Bible: Containing the Old and New Testaments with Apocrypha, Oxford UP,2009.

www.24-7 prayer.com

www.wheaton.edu/ISAE/Defining-Evangelicalism/Pentecostalism

https://en.wikipedia.org/wiki/Confessing Movement

http://www.supersoul.tv/supersoul-sunday/bishop-t-d-jakes-how-to-use-your-time-effectively-and-purposefully

CHAPTER ONE
THE CALL TO FOCUS
NOTES

CHAPTER TWO
FOCUS MOVEMENT
NOTES

CHAPTER THREE
FOCUS IS THE KEY
NOTES

_____
_____
_____
_____
_____
_____
_____
_____
_____
_____

CHAPTER FOUR
SOCIAL MEDIA HELPED DEVELOP DISTRACTIONS
NOTES

CHAPTER FIVE
WHEN DISTRACTED BLINK AND FOCUS

NOTES

_____
_____
_____
_____
_____
_____
_____
_____
_____
_____

CHAPTER SIX
PITFALLS OF WANDERING

NOTES

CHAPTER SEVEN
THE CATERFILLAR UNDERSTANDS FOCUS
NOTES

_____
_____
_____
_____
_____
_____
_____
_____
_____
_____

CHAPTER EIGHT
FOCUS ON THE BODY
NOTES

CHAPTER NINE
TOUGH NATURALLY VS TOFF SPIRITUALLY

NOTES

_____
_____
_____
_____
_____
_____
_____
_____
_____

CHAPTER TEN

IT IS TIME TO SHIFT OUR FOCUS

NOTES

CONCLUSION NOTES

www.ingramcontent.com/pod-product-compliance
Lightning Source LLC
LaVergne TN
LVHW011209080426
835508LV00007B/693